DIFFERENTIATED

DIFFERENTIATED

The Key to Navigating Life in an Exaggerated and Diminished World

THE SERIAL INTELLECTUAL

Innovative Industries 1, LLC

CONTENTS

CHAPTER 1

INTRODUCTION

Prior to being introduced to this book, have you ever heard of the concept of differentiation? It's an unfamiliar concept for most people, though many practice it daily. The term "differentiation" originates from the Latin word *differentia*, which means "difference" or "distinction." This linguistic root emphasizes the core concept of differentiation—making distinctions or identifying differences.

In archaeology, we can trace evidence of differentiation in ancient civilizations. The Sumerians, for instance, used distinct symbols to represent different commodities in their accounting system around 3500 BCE. This early form of differentiation allowed them to track and trade goods effectively, laying the foundation for modern economic systems.

During the Renaissance, differentiation took on new significance in the realm of art and science. Visionaries like Leonardo da Vinci, through his anatomical drawings, and Galileo Galilei, with his telescopic observations, employed differentiation to explore and understand the intricate details of the natural world.

Even in religious texts, such as the *Holy Bible*, differentiation appears as a concept of significance. In the book of Genesis, the story of creation narrates how God differentiated between light and darkness, land and water, and various living creatures. This early reference illustrates the concept's ancient origins and role in explaining life's diversity.

In the annals of American history, the concept of differentiation has also played a pivotal role in shaping the nation's development. Differentiation can be seen from the colonial era through the American Revolution and beyond.

The thirteen American colonies exhibited distinct economic specialties. New England engaged in trade and manufacturing, the Middle Colonies focused on agriculture, and the Southern Colonies relied heavily on plantation-based agriculture, particularly cultivating crops such as tobacco, rice, and indigo. This economic diversity laid the groundwork for regional differentiation in culture and political outlook, which would later influence the course of American history.

Differentiation became a hallmark of political thought and ideology during the American Revolution. The Founding Fathers, including Thomas Jefferson and John Adams, differed in their views on the role of government, individual rights, and the balance of power. These ideological differences ultimately led to the differentiation between the Federalist and Anti-Federalist movements, which, in turn, led to the ratification of the United States Constitution and the Bill of Rights.

The term "differentiation" has evolved over centuries to encapsulate various meanings. Initially rooted in mathematics, it began to find application in various disciplines. In the mid-nineteenth century, mathematicians like Augustin-Louis Cauchy and Karl Weierstrass formalized the concept of differentiation in calculus.

The concept of "differentiated instruction" holds great importance within the field of education, serving as a prominent educational technique. The foundation of this educational framework is based on tailoring instructional methods and educational materials to meet pupils' diverse and specific learning needs. The underlying premise of this approach is that students possess a wide range of abilities, interests, and cognitive tendencies. Differentiated teaching promotes fair learning results by providing several approaches to acquiring knowledge. This approach ensures that the unique learning demands of each student are not only satisfied but also effectively handled.

On the other hand, within business and marketing, the concept of differentiation plays a crucial role as a strategic necessity. Firms and enterprises utilize this strategy to differentiate their products or services from those offered by their competitors in the marketplace. This strategic delineation entails carefully, emphasizing distinct product traits, unique qualities, or a strong branding identity. The primary goal is to infuse the product or service with a natural appeal that powerfully connects with a specific target audience, fostering a competitive edge in the ever-changing field of business.

Imagine standing in a vast field of wildflowers, each of different colors and sizes. Differentiating these flowers means identifying and understanding the unique characteristics that separate each one. This ability to distinguish between the individual flowers in the field represents differentiation in its simplest form.

Differentiation has a crucial role in virtually every subject in the contemporary world. In the field of technology, for example, it is utilized within the domain of computer science to develop algorithms that discern between unsolicited and authentic electronic communications. In marketing, organizations employ brand differentiation as a strategic approach to build distinct identities and effectively appeal to their target client base. Enterprises endeavor to establish a unique selling proposition for their goods and services to distinguish themselves within a highly competitive marketplace. This can encompass the development of distinctive attributes, branding strategies, or customer-centered encounters that distinguish them from their rivals.

Personal branding has become progressively prevalent among individuals to establish a distinctive identity in both professional and personal spheres. Individuals can demonstrate their distinct abilities, specialized knowledge, and personal characteristics to differentiate themselves from prospective employers, clients, or collaborators via social media, blogs, and other digital platforms. The differentiation process holds significant importance for individuals involved in artistic and creative arts, culture, and entertainment endeavors. For instance, individuals engaged in music, literature, and visual arts employ distinctive artistic approaches and expressive techniques to differentiate themselves and establish meaningful connections with their respective audiences.

Differentiation assumes a significant importance within the context of social and political movements. Activists and advocacy groups distinguish themselves by highlighting their distinct objectives, approaches, and communications to mobilize backing for their respective endeavors. Differentiation is also observed in the pursuit of sustainable practices. Business entities and individuals distinguish themselves by embracing environmentally sustainable products and practices to mitigate their impact on the natural environment. Differentiation is also employed in customization algorithms inside the digital domain. Organizations use data to tailor user recommendations and content based on their tastes and behavior.

As we delve deeper into the diverse interpretations and applications of differentiation, we embark on a journey of discovery that enriches our comprehension of the multifaceted world we inhabit and underscores the intrinsic value of recognizing and embracing uniqueness in all its forms. Whether it's the specialized cells in an embryo, the cultural tapestry of humanity, or the distinctive features of products in the marketplace, differentiation is an elemental force that fosters understanding, innovation, and progress in our ever-evolving quest for knowledge and excellence.

Universe

Nature

Humanity

CHAPTER 2

UNIVERSE, NATURE, AND HUMANITY

Universe

Telescopes and scientific research about the universe are of great interest. The James Webb Space Telescope has recently been launched into space and transmits remarkable images and information. The universe exhibits striking diversity, encompassing distinctions in size, planetary composition, rotation, axes, proximity, and galaxies. Consequently, this concept of differentiation is evident both within the universe and our solar system. Various planetary types exist, each characterized by distinct behaviors, rotations, and seemingly evolving purposes that are still being unveiled.

Nature

On Earth, many distinct species exist, each possessing its unique purpose. When visiting a zoo, these distinctions become apparent as lions are grouped with other lions, bears with bears, and penguins inhabiting a colder environment, reflecting our recognition of species differences. Earth also boasts various plants and terrains, marked by climate variations ranging from warm equatorial regions to frigid polar ice caps. Thus, the concept of differentiation is intricately interwoven throughout nature's diverse tapestry.

Every Aspect of Our Humanity

Differentiation is also present in every facet of humanity, including the infrastructure upon which our societies are constructed, such as highways. Distinctions are evident in multiple pathways, entry and exit methods, delineated lines, fast and slow lanes, and carpool lanes, which are restricted unless occupied by at least two individuals.

The concept of differentiation is abundantly evident across all our systems, with education as a prime example. As mentioned previously, education is arguably at the forefront of embracing differentiation, closely followed by science, which employs a differentiated teaching model to acknowledge individual student progress.

Additionally, differentiation is observable within our government, particularly in the West, especially in the United States. Here, we have three branches of government: the executive branch, the legislative branch, and the judicial branch, each with distinct functions and inherent differences. These distinctions are evident within the government structure and extend to political parties, various roles in politics and government, and the unique authority vested in each position.

Furthermore, differentiation permeates our relationships with distinctions based on gender, age, abilities, and skills. These categories shape the dynamics within our relationships, whether between parents and children or among individuals, affecting the outcomes and practical interactions among them.

The final context where differentiation is evident within humanity lies in our bodies. Our bodies consist of numerous distinct parts, and when in good health, these components collaborate toward a common purpose despite their differences. An ancient text conveys that no part, such as the eye or the hand, can claim it doesn't require the other parts, like the heart. They all function together, despite their differences, to achieve a collective goal.

How Vital Is Differentiation?

Differentiation is needed in various aspects of our lives. Consider our bodies, where vital organs like the brain, heart, and lungs are indispensable components, without which we cannot thrive. Similarly, differentiation is a fundamental necessity. The practice of differentiation is essential to lead healthy, complete, and functional lives. It can be described as an absolute requirement for existence, deeply ingrained in our DNA and evident in our bodies, universe, nature, systems, and structures.

CHAPTER 3

DRAMA

For the sake of this chapter we are going to define the term "drama" as an unwavering dedication to relational dysfunction. Often, this word is casually used to broadly label situations perceived as excessive, exaggerated, or troublesome.

A significant portion of the drama we encounter serves as a protective mechanism for individuals. In essence, some people employ drama to maintain a safe distance from intimacy. When there's an abundance of drama, it tends to deter people from getting close, resulting in them maintaining a distance. Drama often causes offense, hurt feelings, and uncomfortable situations. However, employing differentiation when dealing with drama signifies a desire to comprehend it, to pose inquiries about it, and to examine its make-up. This approach proves particularly beneficial in understanding and managing drama on a deeper level.

Another way in which differentiation proves beneficial when dealing with drama is by determining which aspects of drama warrant attention and resolution and which may be unnecessary to address. A practical way to implement differentiation when dealing with drama is to ask straightforward questions like "Why is it consistently happening?" and "Is there anything about the circumstances that lend to producing drama?" This differentiated approach allows you to navigate your way through the exaggerations and diminishments of drama. It will also enable you to comprehend the relational dynamics so that you can pursue a path that is more likely to end in win win situations for everyone.

One of the things that happens when you engage in a differentiated approach is that it helps you to gain a holistic understanding of an individual. As fallible individuals, we can enter phases or be influenced by our predispositions, past experiences, wounds, or weaknesses, leading us to display hurtful and challenging traits. But, even in all of this people are capable of transformation and doing good. Someone lacking differentiation will fail to recognize this aspect and only perceive the negative, potentially missing an opportunity to relate to someone in a different and more meaningful way.

Additionally, differentiation benefits not only individuals but also organizations and institutions, which routinely contend with drama. In a differentiated context, there's a willingness to pose challenging questions about drama, whether directed inwardly or at the organization itself. These questions will incite a corporate self-reflection, a closer look at all the contributing factors that shape things, and an understanding of the perspectives and objectives of individuals or groups involved. This mindset allows organizations to dissect any situation's multifaceted components, providing a framework for discerning what merits attention and what can be disregarded.

CHAPTER 4

RELIGION

Differentiation is seen in all of the world's religions. This may come as a shock to many of you because religion is often presented to us as a system of beliefs and behaviors which have little to no nuance. But, a close examination of most of the world's religions will show you that they all contain differentiation in their DNA. I would like to add something right here for your consideration while we are on this topic. It is my personal belief and experience that those who practice differentiation with their faith are more likely to have a better experience with it, influence more people through it and remain committed to it.

I would like to give you an illustration of differentiation within religion. There is a verse from the New Testament of the *Holy Bible*, located in Romans 12:9, which says, "abhor what is evil and cling to what is good." This verse is a compelling example of differentiation. It acknowledges the existence of evil and good within the Christian worldview. Notice, it does not advocate focusing solely on one aspect but directs Christians to engage in two actions, necessitating differentiation simultaneously. Again, this is where individuals who practice a religion, irrespective of their faith, often err in my opinion. They focus on one part of their faith and not the other. And, the reason why they tend to do this is because it is what is taught and rewarded. However, it is very clear from this verse that if a person adheres to the Christian faith and its teachings they should be embracing and practicing both at the same time.

This can be challenging for religious practitioners because we prefer clarity and binary distinctions over ambiguity. While this scripture's teaching is not ambiguous, its application can appear gray because it requires the simultaneous practice of two distinct actions. And, this can be challenging for religious individuals. They tend to adopt certain beliefs and incorporate specific practices but often overlook the holistic integration of their religion, which would necessitate differentiation.

Another reason why some people find differentiation difficult to practice with religion is because of the perception that it is a compromise to faith itself. When they hear the concept they think it is asking them to dismiss or deny an aspect of their faith. Nothing could be further from the truth! It is actually the exact opposite. It is asking them to incorporate the totality of their faith. In fact, individuals who are religious but lack differentiation in their approach to religion often exhibit exaggerated and diminished and potentially harmful practices, making them some of the most hurtful and destructive individuals on the planet. Anyone who wants to demonstrate the benefits of their religion, encourage others to embrace their faith, and desire it to be more accessible and acceptable to those who do not share their beliefs, should practice it in a differentiated manner.

Another benefit of practicing differentiation in a religious context is that it enables us to see that many religions share common tenets, beliefs, and principles. The point here is not to suggest that adherents of a particular faith become universalists and cease distinguishing or recognizing the distinctions between their religion and others. The point is that differentiation can aid individuals in recognizing that common bonds and principles are frequently present in other religions. The question that someone may ask at this point is "Why is this important?"

I see at least three reasons why it's important. First, it can help us to clarify our own beliefs and practices which should lead to us embodying our own religion in a more authentic manner. Second, it can show us where there's common ground in our beliefs and practices, thus promoting collaboration when it's possible. Third, it can help you respect and love people who practice different religions. Differentiation allows me to explore areas of agreement and at the same time respectfully acknowledge areas of disagreement. It encourages me to disagree as amicably as possible.

CHAPTER 5

POLITICS

While the principles I discuss in this book generally apply to individuals in any part of the world and within any governmental system, most of my examples will be drawn from the American political framework. This choice does not indicate a belief that the American system is superior in all cases, nor does it imply a lack of awareness regarding other systems. Rather, I utilize the American system for illustration and application because it aligns with my familiarity as a longtime student of political studies and facilitates effective communication of differentiation concepts within the American political context.

In the realm of politics, differentiation can play a pivotal role. If a commitment to practicing differentiation were established, approximately 90 percent of the political dysfunction currently prevalent in American culture would swiftly dissipate. The root cause, as previously discussed in an earlier chapter, lies in the failure to embrace differentiation, which results in an exaggerated and intensified bias. This bias is evident in contemporary politics, within the United States and in numerous other nations.

When consistent harm is inflicted upon people through policies that are purportedly in their best interest but, in reality, are detrimental, it inevitably sparks rebellion, the emergence of alternative political movements, antagonistic responses from other parties, or similar events. A shift towards oppressive measures may occur to remain in power under such circumstances, a phenomenon observable worldwide. However, a commitment to differentiation can bring about a different scenario. In such a context, individuals with diverse perspectives would engage in constructive dialogues, acknowledging, with humility, their disagreements on various policies and differing perceptions. Nonetheless, they would also identify common ground. This concept is referred to as bipartisanship in American politics and its two-party political system.

Bipartisanship is a term commonly invoked during reelection season, with candidates emphasizing their ability to collaborate and work across political divides. However, the unfortunate reality is that once elections conclude, bipartisanship often dwindles, particularly in social media and news outlets. Instead, it gives way to amplified biases detrimental to political parties and those living within those systems, whether in the United States or elsewhere. The consistent outcome of this shift is harm and damage. The only means by which the party in power can maintain its position is through power grabs and authoritarian actions, which are detrimental to any nation.

In contemporary politics worldwide, differentiation is arguably the most essential and valuable tool. It involves the capacity to engage with political opponents, identifying areas of agreement and common interests. However, a challenge arises when practicing differentiation, as it presupposes the ability to perceive multiple perspectives. In practice, this requires individuals to differentiate themselves. Regrettably, not everyone possesses this trait; irrespective of statistics, historical facts, public opinion, or evidence, some individuals remain unwavering in their commitment to their chosen path, impervious to external influence.

In such cases, differentiation is ineffective, and the only recourse may be a social revolution—a regrettable reality. Practicing differentiation in politics requires engaging with individuals who possess internal differentiation, individuals capable of humility and cooperation despite disagreements on specific issues. This collaboration aims at the collective welfare of the people and can be highly beneficial.

Additionally, differentiation becomes essential if one aligns with and pledges loyalty to a particular political party. No single political party can claim absolute authority on truth and governance practices. While some parties may excel in certain areas, it is rare in human history for any one party or political perspective to consistently serve the people's best interests across all domains.

Differentiation requires individuals who align with political parties to remain open-minded and acknowledge that their political affiliation does not equate to unwavering support for every aspect of the party or candidate's stance. It implies a readiness to admit that some aspects need improvement and a willingness to work toward that change actively. It also entails the courage to address issues directly and honestly. However, the reality is that in the current political landscape, differentiation needs to be incentivized or rewarded.

Individuals who exhibit differentiation often become targets of persecution, facing consequences such as cancellation, marginalization, labeling, and name-calling. This is an unfortunate reality in our current political climate. However, despite these challenges, embracing differentiation is one of the most valuable things for individuals, political parties, and our culture. The ability to say "I may not agree with this person's beliefs on certain issues, but on others, they are correct," and finding ways to collaborate on common ground can be immensely beneficial. Without this willingness to differentiate in our political approach, we will continue to experience political dysfunction.

How could we see differentiation as a practice increase in our political environments? By creating better systems of accountability for all politicians, while at the same time having severe consequences for those who refuse to practice it and rewards for those who promote it. There needs to be more incentive for the leaders of our political parties to promote, practice and embody differentiation because the unfortunate reality of today's political climate is that those who move towards differentiation often suffer the loss of their influence, power and position. Therefore, it's rare to find a leader who is willing to practice this. The increase in a differentiated approach in politics will never come from the top. If we are every going to see it it will come from the grassroots level. If we, as a society, culture, communities, nations, and civilians, desire a more differentiated approach to politics, we must work toward it actively. This requires a few crucial steps.

First, we must stop blindly accepting the political ideologies presented to us and instead approach our choices with a discerning mindset. This means considering why we vote for specific candidates and critically analyzing our decisions rather than merely adhering to tradition or upbringing. Secondly, we must establish mechanisms for holding those in positions of power accountable. It's important to note that individuals with authority and influence are often reluctant to relinquish it voluntarily. Consequently, implementing these changes will take a lot of work. Nevertheless, if we genuinely desire a more differentiated political landscape, the impetus must come from the grassroots, from us.

Achieving accountability in politics, particularly for leaders who don't practice differentiation, necessitates taking action. In some global political systems where the population needs a voice and influence, this might seem attainable by resorting to social revolution. However, in systems where citizen engagement and influence are possible, it entails leaving behind political apathy and becoming active participants. To bring about change, people must support candidates who embrace differentiation and endorse policies that require a differentiated approach. This proactive stance is vital for holding politicians accountable and promoting a more differentiated political landscape.

Consider the scenario where a city official is tasked with determining the optimal taxation strategy for its citizens. Instead of relying on an individual's judgment, a more differentiated approach could involve establishing a council or cabinet composed of elected representatives collaborating with the elected official. However, this transformation is only possible with active advocacy and community-driven efforts to demand policies or legislation incorporating diverse perspectives. This entails a wake-up call, a departure from our habitual voting patterns, and the need to employ strategic measures such as fiscal or institutional boycotts to capture politicians attention and compel them to return to the negotiation table. For instance, students dissatisfied with a school policy can orchestrate a walkout to effect change. However, for such actions to be effective, they must inflict significant consequences, possibly by extending the walkout duration to several days, thus diminishing school attendance and financial support. In many American schools, funding is contingent upon student attendance.

This concept is transferable to government scenarios. For example, if you reside in a city where you're dissatisfied with the unjust approach of the justice system, consistently favoring criminals, you may need to employ a tactic like a fiscal boycott. If a significant portion of the city's population participates in such a boycott, it would undoubtedly capture the attention of the leaders.

CHAPTER 6

SOCIAL MEDIA

Differentiation is valuable in helping us to navigate the exaggerated and diminished world of social media. It is arguably the most powerful influence in most people's lives. Understanding differentiation would empower us with a newfound discernment so that we can distinguish between authentic information and content that helps us, and disingenuous information that is primarily made to enslave us! Consequently, we would be better equipped to make informed decisions about what we engage with and invest in.

Furthermore, it's essential to acknowledge that, despite exposure to individuals on social media who may appear exceptionally successful, the truth is most people don't fall into that category. Differentiation encourages us to grasp this truth and aids us in recognizing that the landscape of social media mirrors the broader world we inhabit. Therefore, we don't need to internalize negative energy or develop false perceptions of ourselves when we engage it.

It's also crucial to teach our children how to apply differentiation when they use social media, and we should promote differentiation within our families and friendships in the context of social media usage. We should never relinquish one of our most precious gifts, the freedom to choose and determine the extent to which something influences us. While we may not always have control over our exposure to various content, we consistently maintain control over our responses. This embodies a differentiated approach to social media.

Furthermore, it's essential to acknowledge that, despite the significance of social media in today's world, most people live outside of it, largely unaffected by its presence. Many of these individuals lead successful and content lives. A differentiated approach to social media prevents us from becoming overly absorbed in a world that often portrays social media as the only way to live. It reminds us that there is more to life than what is depicted on on-screen or in streams.

CHAPTER 7

LEADERSHIP

Differentiation holds substantial value for leaders as it helps them to understand the distinctions between what they lead, who they lead and how they lead. When leaders don't practice this it tends to open the door for a lot of dysfunction.

Some companies and organizations are driven by the pressure to achieve specific outcomes and may prioritize them above all else. However, for those seeking a comprehensive and sustainable leadership experience while increasing the likelihood of effectiveness, it is essential to recognize that the "how" and "who" of leadership carries equal weight to the "what." Leadership inherently entails responsibility, and a true leader assumes all associated liabilities while generously sharing credit. Therefore, differentiation is paramount when assessing the organization and fellow leaders or individuals within it. Moreover, differentiation is crucial when evaluating other leaders as a leader yourself. It allows you to recognize that you will naturally be more inclined toward certain individuals, forming closer connections and personal preferences.

However, a differentiated approach allows us to acknowledge that even if we don't have a personal affinity for someone, they may excel in their work. It enables us to ask essential questions such as "What's the goal?" and "What's the mission?" and to separate personal feelings from the broader objectives. From an organizational perspective, we should adopt a differentiated approach when choosing leaders. Frequently, we depend on predefined criteria and a specific set of qualifications, and while this approach isn't fundamentally flawed, we search for individuals who merely meet these checkboxes.

A differentiated approach suggests that if there are ten criteria to be met and a candidate fulfills only seven, it raises the question of whether they can acquire the skills required for the remaining three over the next six months or a year. Could they eventually evolve into a highly capable leader? In essence, it's about considering the bigger picture. A differentiated approach, like observing a butterfly larva, understands that it's not a butterfly at the moment but has the potential to become one. Too often, organizations make leadership choices driven by exaggerated biases or historical precedents rather than adopting a differentiated and objective stance to identify the best candidate for the role given the specific circumstances. A differentiated approach can guide an organization in making more informed decisions.

While I was leading a church years ago I led our staff through an Enneagram personality assessment. Through the Enneagram assessments we identified that some of our staff relied heavily on their feelings to do relationships, while others approached situations more intellectually. I belong to the category of instinct-driven individuals. During one particular meeting, we discussed updates to our security measures. I expressed concern that our facility was vulnerable and anyone could potentially steal the new equipment we had recently installed. Present at the meeting were two members of the building's security team, both highly analytical and prone to anxiety.

During the meeting I had made a statement suggesting that the facility was vulnerable to anyone walking in and taking items. The security team took this statement literally and locked down the building. I returned the following week and found the building locked down. Those in charge of the building had implemented new security measures seeking to ensure that my scenario would not happen. They made new keys for every door and had spreadsheets, all of which struck me as inefficient and cumbersome. Honestly, I was frustrated with them.

However, my perspective changed when I spoke with another leader who approached situations with differentiation.

The differentiated leader helped me see that my statement had triggered their fears, leading them to secure the building for peace of mind. This experience taught me the importance of a differentiated approach, which focuses on getting the job done while seeking to understand individuals so that as a leader, I can assist them in performing their roles more effectively. It highlighted the need for improved communication that avoids absolute or hyperbolic statements.

CHAPTER 8

LIMITATIONS AND LOSSES

When you embrace differentiation, you can perceive various facets of your experiences. One crucial aspect is recognizing that limitations and losses are an inevitable part of life. They are inherent realities that everyone faces. Differentiation helps you understand that these limitations and losses do not define your identity. Instead, they are events or circumstances that happen to you but do not encompass the entirety of who you are.

In contrast, a non-differentiated perspective might lead to the belief that if you encounter limitations and losses in your personal life—relationships, family, parenting, career, community, or social media—it must reflect something negative about your character or worth. However, a differentiated mindset allows you to discern that these challenges do not directly reflect your identity.

This mindset embraces the universality of these challenges, recognizing that they are part of the shared human experience. Moreover, it emphasizes that limitations and losses should not be uniformly categorized as negative. On the other hand, while certain events like the loss of a loved one or a battle with a severe terminal illness certainly bring sorrow, many such life experiences serve as catalysts for personal growth and transformation. They act as helpful forces, propelling us to shift our routines, adapt our rhythms, and break free from stagnant life phases. Furthermore, they encourage us to overcome obstacles, inviting others to support us and fostering a culture of greater vulnerability and connection.

Limitations and losses serve as reminders to work more efficiently, not just harder. They create a sense of urgency, for we know these inevitable challenges lie in wait, with uncertain timing. As a result, we understand the significance of seizing the present moment, recognizing that it might be our last chance to engage in activities like writing, cycling, or expressing love to a loved one. A differentiated approach considers these realities holistically, acknowledging their undeniable presence.

A differentiated approach to navigating life, especially during unexpected setbacks or losses, involves using a wide-angle lens, a telescope, and a microscope simultaneously. When viewing life solely through a microscope, one tends to focus exclusively on the tiniest details of a setback or loss, which can lead to misery. However, a differentiated perspective acknowledges the importance of incorporating a telescope, allowing one to see beyond the minutiae and gain a broader outlook.

While the microscope may lead to self-doubt and self-criticism, the telescope allows you to look into the future and recognize the vast array of opportunities and possibilities awaiting you. For instance, losing a job or ending a relationship might trigger microscopic self-reflection, questioning what went wrong. However, a telescopic view reminds you that the world is filled with billions of people and countless opportunities in the days, months, and years ahead.

A differentiated mindset also incorporates the wide-angle lens to gain a broader perspective on the surrounding circumstances. Moreover, it acknowledges the value of seeking insights from friends and loved ones who can offer unique perspectives and support during challenging times. This comprehensive approach guides one's feelings, thoughts, processes, and actions to navigate and overcome unexpected setbacks and losses in life.

CHAPTER 9

LOVE

Differentiation underscores the idea that love is a dynamic force encompassing both changeable and unchangeable aspects. In the intricate web of human relationships, love often finds itself subject to shifts and fluctuations as circumstances evolve. Differentiated individuals exhibit a keen awareness of these changes and possess the capacity to adapt their expressions of love accordingly. Conversely, differentiation also recognizes that there are instances where love demands a steadfast, unchanging expression, exemplified by a parent's unwavering affection for their child.

The way in which love is bestowed upon a child is profoundly influenced by their growth, actions, and the ever-evolving dynamics of the parent-child relationship. Differentiated individuals possess the discernment to navigate these distinctions, adjusting their expressions of love in alignment with the unique needs of each phase. This ability to adapt their love according to the evolving nature of relationships fosters deeper connections and stronger bonds.

Furthermore, differentiation provides a lens through which one can comprehend the concept of seasons within love. 'Love, like the changing seasons, experiences a multitude of phases—from the initial spark of infatuation to the enduring warmth of ardor, from the challenges of collusion to the liberating abandon of reckless love, and even from the strategic considerations of love to the intentional cultivation of love through detailed plans. Love, much like the natural world, adapts to the seasons marked by periods of ample time spent together or scarce moments, abundant resources, or limited means. Differentiated individuals possess an acute awareness of these subtle transitions and artfully incorporate them into their approach to love. This dynamic approach allows love to thrive and flourish even amidst changing circumstances.

One of the most profound lessons of differentiation is its ability to clarify that the outcomes of love do not define one's core identity. Regardless of how one loves or the results that love yields, an individual's fundamental identity remains immutable. There are moments when one may excel in expressing love, yet the external results may not mirror this effort. Conversely, one might receive an abundance of love but find it challenging to accept or reciprocate due to complicating factors. Differentiation underscores that these outcomes are extrinsic to one's self; they are mere consequences of the interplay between individuals and circumstances. Individuals who practice differentiation can disentangle their sense of self from the outcomes of their love experiences, finding solace and a deeper sense of self-worth within the constancy of their core identity. This insight liberates individuals from the weight of external judgments, allowing them to engage in love with a sense of authenticity and freedom.

CHAPTER 10

PSYCHOLOGY

Delving into the interplay between differentiation and psychology unveils a multifaceted landscape where the first crucial key point emerges: the integral role of thoughts within one's identity. It's important to recognize that the significance of thoughts within one's identity can vary depending on an individual's psychological tendencies. For those who tend to embark on introspective journeys, contemplation forms a substantial component of their existence. In contrast, individuals primarily driven by emotions or instincts may find this concept less directly applicable. However, a fundamental truth remains—thoughts represent only one facet of a person's identity. A differentiated individual possesses the wisdom to understand this and they can skillfully manage, moderate, listen to, and satisfy these thoughts without succumbing to their overpowering influence.

Moreover, differentiation provides a powerful lens through which to understand the purpose behind our thoughts. Many of our thoughts are deeply rooted in survival instincts designed to keep us alive and safeguarded from potential threats. Others serve as motivational beacons, propelling us forward on our life journeys. As one embraces differentiation within the realm of psychology, a profound realization dawns. Every thought possesses a "why," a reason and a purpose. These thoughts are not random or arbitrary; they are intricately connected to our innate drive for survival, well-being, and progress.

A third pivotal facet of differentiation within psychology is the recognition that all thoughts have an origin story. Each thought, no matter how fleeting or profound, can be traced back to its birthplace within our psyche. This exploration allows for a deeper understanding of why our thoughts manifest as they do and where they originate. It unravels the intricate tapestry of our psychological landscape, shedding light on the forces that shape our cognitive processes.

URE

CHAPTER 11

PAST

It's essential to grasp that despite the formidable influence of the past, it's not the sole tense shaping your life. A differentiated individual recognizes that life is comprised of three tenses: the past, the present, and the future. In a sense, one possesses three selves: a past self, a present self, and a future self. To ensure personal well-being, these three selves must understand each other and collaborate, as my book on *tenses* emphasized.

Differentiation can assist you in dealing with your past by repositioning it. Regardless of the events and experiences that have unfolded, your past can be repositioned or redeemed to serve your interests rather than hinder them. Achieving this transformation requires intentionality, substantial effort, and the willingness to confront uncomfortable thoughts and emotions. A differentiated approach to the past acknowledges that it's a component of our existence that has transpired but does not encompass our entirety. We can bring our past into the present and harness its potential to improve our future. Adopting a differentiated approach helps you understand that it does not define you. Instead, it represents the voice from your past self that whispers guidance to your current self. While we may not always control our experiences, we invariably possess the power to dictate how we interpret and respond to them. Differentiated individuals are keenly aware of this fact and apply it to their relationship with the past.

CHAPTER 12

GENDER

Gender is an undeniably sensitive subject of great significance in today's world. It has sparked numerous debates and discussions across various platforms, including in-person seminars, conferences within religious institutions, political arenas, universities conducting research, and prominently on social media. Nevertheless, the concept of differentiation can play a pivotal role in enhancing these crucial conversations. When we grasp the essence of differentiation, which involves discerning differences, it can guide us toward progress in our contemporary world.

Differentiation encourages us to see individuals holistically, comprehend all their attributes and recognize their inherent worth. Ultimately, regardless of where individuals stand on gender issues, their humanity remains unchanged. They retain their intrinsic value, deserve to be treated with dignity, and merit our respect. Furthermore, it is evident that men and women have ontological similarities and differences. A differentiated approach acknowledges both without exaggerating or diminishing either one.

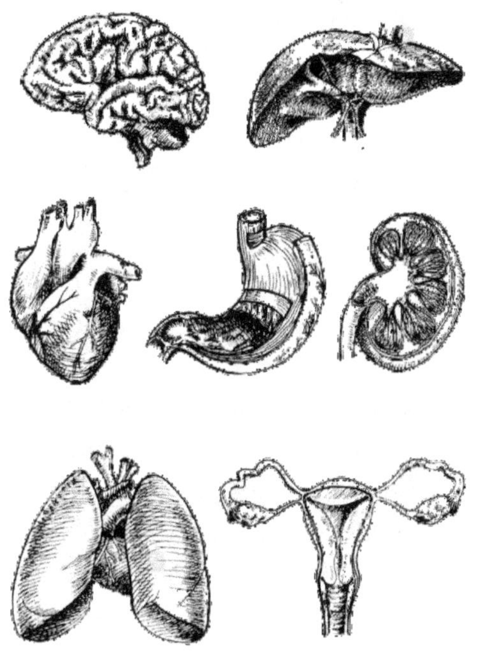

CHAPTER 13

INTERNAL SYSTEMS

Human beings are made up of physical and immaterial components. The physical components include organs, bones, and muscles, while the immaterial components include our emotions, thoughts, and soul. Both aspects shape our identity and experiences.

Differentiation serves as a powerful lens through which we can discern the boundaries that separate these facets and explore their incredible capacity for collaboration. This collaboration can manifest in myriad ways, influencing our overall well-being and contributing to positive or negative outcomes.

Within the field of psychology, the internal family systems approach serves as a guiding light for individuals seeking to navigate the intricacies of their internal makeup. This approach encourages individuals to look into their psyches, peeling back the layers to identify all the internal elements at play and evaluate their proper functionality. It's important to note that these elements within our immaterial composition are not static; they can assume various roles and states, becoming amplified or diminished in significance, taking on protective roles in response to trauma or stress, or even being relegated to the background or suppressed altogether.

Moreover, the application of differentiation extends beyond the realm of psychology to the domain of physical health. Physicians and healthcare professionals, in their assessments of our physical condition, find differentiation to be a valuable tool. By recognizing the various components within our physical composition and understanding how they interact, medical practitioners can diagnose and treat various health issues more effectively. This nuanced approach enables them to address immediate concerns and empowers individuals to make informed decisions about their health and well-being, fostering a sense of agency and partnership in the healing process.

CHAPTER 14

FAMILY

Differentiation is a profound concept that can significantly enrich the dynamics of a family unit, primarily by creating a space for individuality to flourish within the embrace of a communal framework. This aspect of family life, discussed earlier in this book, underscores the idea that authenticity need not clash with familial norms; rather, it encourages individuals to manifest their true selves within the context of their family's established values and traditions. By adopting a differentiated approach to family dynamics, one can effectively hold principles and individuality in equilibrium, allowing them to coexist harmoniously. This balance brings solace to family members and fosters unity and motivation within the family structure.

Within a differentiated family, there is room for the collective principles that bind the family together and individual family members' unique expressions of these principles. This perspective recognizes that while a family may hold steadfast to certain guiding principles, the interpretation and application of these principles can vary significantly from one family member to another. For instance, a family may value education as a core principle, but each member might approach their educational journey in distinctive ways, pursuing different fields of study or career paths. This diversity in interpretation and application reflects the richness of individuality within the family and reinforces its principles of adaptability and resilience.

One of the most significant benefits of a differentiated approach to family life is the sense of solace it brings to its members. Knowing that one can authentically express oneself while adhering to family values creates a profound inner peace. This is especially valuable in a world that often pressures individuals to conform to societal expectations or rebel against their family's traditions. In a differentiated family, unity is not achieved by stifling individuality but by celebrating it. Family members learn to appreciate and respect each other's unique perspectives and paths, fostering a deep sense of connection and support.

Moreover, differentiation within a family serves as a wellspring of encouragement. When family members see others pursuing their authentic paths while respecting the family's principles, it inspires them to do the same. This mutual support system encourages personal growth and development, as family members feel empowered to explore their interests and ambitions without fear of judgment or rejection.

In essence, differentiation offers a delicate yet powerful balance between tradition and individuality within a family. It reinforces the idea that family can be a source of strength, nurturing the identity and potential of each member while preserving the family's core values. By embracing differentiation, families can thrive as cohesive units where authenticity, unity, and encouragement coexist, fostering a deep sense of belonging and fulfillment for all.

CHAPTER 15

MARRIAGE

Marriage, often regarded as one of the closest and most intimate relationships, is a crucible in which profound insights about ourselves and our partners are continually unearthed. It is a unique space where our true selves are unveiled, sometimes in ways that surprise and challenge us. In this context, differentiation becomes a valuable tool for navigating the complexities of married life.

Within the framework of marriage, differentiation takes on a crucial role by helping us dissect the origins of our experiences in relationships. It equips us to distinguish between intrinsic characteristics, external influences, and potentially detrimental behaviors. Rather than interpreting our partner's actions, a differentiated approach urges us to examine these experiences through a multifaceted lens. It encourages us to consider whether our partner's behaviors and reactions may be rooted in personal wounds, vulnerabilities, or other underlying factors.

Indeed, the wellspring of experiences in a marital relationship can be diverse, spanning from deep-seated personal wounds and vulnerabilities to potentially harmful intentions. Failing to embrace differentiation in marriage can have adverse consequences, particularly given the importance of intimacy within this relationship.

Differentiation empowers individuals to dissect the various layers of their experiences within this relationship, ultimately fostering empathy, understanding, and resilience. By recognizing the multifaceted nature of human behavior and motivation, couples can forge deeper connections and navigate the challenges of married life with greater wisdom and compassion.

ACQUISITION

What steps can individuals and communities take to ensure that differentiation is present and effective in their daily lives?

Step number one involves making a commitment to listen effectively. A practical gauge of your listening skills is the ability to repeat what the other person said and ensure they concur with your understanding. Step two, see the importance of asking numerous questions, recognizing that we have two ears and one mouth, indicating the need to listen more than we speak. Step three calls for individuals and communities to prioritize differentiation and its practice as a core value in their relationships, striving for it daily.

Are there any strategies or best practices to promote differentiation?

First, create an inclusive environment where everyone, especially those who are typically reserved, are encouraged to voice their opinions without fear of retribution. Second, leaders bear the responsibility of promoting these best practices and ensuring their adoption across various settings, be it in the home, workplace, or any institution. Third, demonstrate the benefits of differentiation to instill a desire for its practice among individuals. Finally, provide education on the subject to ensure everyone is well-informed about what differentiation entails and how to apply it in their lives.

What are the prerequisites for experiencing differentiation?

Humility is crucial in any context, whether it's between individuals, within a family, an organization, or society. Differentiation often stirs strong emotions and disagreements, and humility serves as the binding force that acknowledges the importance of others. Secondly, a commitment to preserving dignity must underpin our interactions, especially when navigating the challenges that differentiation can bring. Every individual should be treated with respect, even in moments of disagreement. Thirdly, creating a safe and supportive culture is vital because differentiation requires vulnerability, and people will only open up when they feel secure.

How does one acquire the skill and knowledge to practice differentiation more effectively?

Reading, especially books that tackle complex subjects, can be highly beneficial. Such books expand your thinking and often present differentiated perspectives. Exposing yourself to debates is valuable. Debates involve two sides striving to comprehend each other's viewpoints to highlight weaknesses or establish the superiority of their own stance, inherently involving differentiation. Practice differentiation in your relationships and environments by actively asking questions and follow-up questions. Additionally, observing individuals who possess this skill and emulating their approach can be instructive.

CHAPTER 16

QUESTION AND ANSWER

How can differentiation help me with my personal or professional development?

The first thing we need to do is define what personal development is. Personal development is an intentional and strategic process where an individual experiences growth in self-awareness, relational aptitude, personal skills, vocational effectiveness and fulfillment in life.

Now that we have a working definition, here are 3 ways it could help you. First, it encourages you to undergo an assessment prior to starting your development journey in order to discover who you are. Second, it could help you to see that your individuality and uniqueness necessitates a customized plan in order to make your development process more effective. Third, it could help you regulate your emotions and thoughts as you experience outcomes.

Can you provide examples of differentiation in the business world, especially in terms of product or service offerings?

In business, differentiation is evident through companies' laser-like focus on their target audience. Businesses often concentrate on specific age demographics or particular problems that require solutions. For instance, in a recent conversation with a family member contemplating starting a technology-related business, they expressed a desire to help solve people's technological problems. I pointed out that this goal needed to be more specific. Which technological problem was their product going to solve? For whom?

A differentiated approach urges us to think critically about the individuals we aim to serve and the products or services we intend to create, pinpointing our precise audience. In this case, I recommended they identify a specific age group, particularly the elderly in our society, who face unique technology-related challenges. This example underscores the importance of businesses being well-understood and resistant to misinterpretation.

What are some common challenges or barriers to achieving differentiation in a workplace or organization, and how can they be overcome?

The most significant challenge or barrier is undoubtedly the organizational culture. Culture encompasses the subtle, intangible, yet palpable presence of values and behaviors. When a workplace culture does not prioritize differentiation, it becomes exceedingly difficult to implement it. Many organizations are highly outcome-oriented, with established systems and structures geared toward achieving specific results. Consequently, differentiation may only be a prominent aspect of the workplace at the leadership level, as front-line employees typically have well-defined roles and expectations.

While culture poses a substantial challenge, human nature also presents hurdles. Most individuals prefer routine and predictability in their workplaces. We thrive on established rhythms and habits, knowing what is expected. Healthy organizations and workplaces typically operate with well-defined values, systems, and structures that guide daily practices. Employees understand what constitutes success and failure within these frameworks.

However, the danger lies in organizations becoming overly focused on routine tasks and "checking the boxes," neglecting to think innovatively about outcomes, inputs, and strategies that could enhance the organization's overall performance. Another significant challenge to differentiation is resistance to change, a characteristic often deeply rooted within workplaces and organizations. Change is frequently met with resistance as it disrupts established routines, necessitates new learning, and introduces unfamiliar challenges. Since the practice of differentiation often demands change in various aspects, it naturally faces resistance due to our inherent aversion to change.

What role does differentiation play in fostering creativity and innovation in various fields, such as technology, arts, or science?

Differentiation acknowledges individuals with diverse skill sets and passions within a given context. It endeavors to create an environment that accommodates and nurtures these passions and skills, enabling individuals to thrive in their areas of expertise. Furthermore, differentiation seeks to establish a framework for personal development, encompassing infrastructure and systems that facilitate continuous growth throughout individuals' careers. This approach is particularly crucial in technology, arts, and science. When subjected to rigid and regimented approaches, these fields are susceptible to stagnation, especially when they become closely affiliated with large corporations or government entities.

Differentiation can be likened to fertilizer in technology, arts, and science. Removing it, whether for messaging purposes, political agendas, or profit motives, can stunt creativity. Creativity inherently involves thinking within and outside established norms or boxes. Thus, it is imperative to acknowledge that some individuals excel within the box while others thrive outside of it. Creating an environment that embraces and encourages both approaches fosters creativity and innovation.

Can differentiation be overemphasized or misapplied? Are there situations where a more uniform approach might be preferable?

Like any other concept, differentiation can be exaggerated and diminished. When exaggerated, it tends to transform our distinctions into perceived deficiencies. Conversely, when diminished, it neglects to acknowledge our distinctions and accentuates our commonalities, erasing humanity's unique creative aspects.

The primary way differentiation is prone to be overemphasized and misapplied manifest through exaggeration and diminishment. This phenomenon is evident in numerous contemporary examples. An illustrative instance lies in the differentiation between race and ethnicity. Differentiation encourages us to recognize that, as human beings, we share an extensive array of common traits and attributes to the extent that our commonalities far outnumber our differences, which primarily manifest in our cultural and ethnic backgrounds.

However, overemphasizing differentiation can lead to an undue emphasis on cultural and ethnic disparities to the detriment of recognizing our shared human race. Conversely, it can also result in an overemphasis on race, thereby downplaying the significance of cultural distinctions. This tension often plays out across various arenas, such as society, politics, religion, philosophy, and social media, and is readily observable by those who pay attention.

Therefore, individuals must apply differentiation thoughtfully and avoid falling into the traps of either overemphasis or misapplication. Striking a balance between uniformity and creativity is achievable, as these concepts need not conflict. While certain uniform principles, such as compassion and nonviolence, are necessary for the well-being of individuals, families, and societies, they can coexist harmoniously with creativity and differences. Differentiation should not unnecessarily pit uniformity against creativity or differences; they can complement each other effectively.

How does differentiation contribute to diversity and inclusion efforts in workplaces and society?

Differentiation within the workplace and society involves recognizing our commonalities while acknowledging individuals' diverse contributions. A differentiating approach aims to create room for these diverse contributions, naturally fostering inclusivity. However, a persistent challenge arises when individuals, whether their reasons are just or unjust, reasonable or unreasonable, believe that accommodating specific people, viewpoints, or lifestyles may adversely affect other perspectives, paradigms, or ways of life. This challenge reflects the complexity of human nature, and it is unlikely that a definitive solution will ever be reached. Nonetheless, upholding universal, transcendent rights for all individuals is crucial as long as mutual respect and unharmful interactions are maintained and individuals are not compelled to act against their genuine desires.

What is the future of differentiation, and how might it evolve or become more important in the coming years, given societal and technological changes?

Never before have we been exposed to such vast ideas and narratives concerning how we should perceive and navigate life. In light of this, differentiation is becoming increasingly essential for our future. This heightened importance arises from our contemporary ability to disseminate global messages in previously inconceivable ways. Messages originating in the United States can now reach and impact individuals worldwide, reflecting the globalization of our interconnected world. This phenomenon was far less prevalent a mere decade or two ago.

The significance of differentiation is underscored by our innate desire for acceptance and affiliation with the prevailing ideologies. As particular perspectives or opinions gain popularity and viral momentum, people often tend to align themselves with these prevailing views, assuming that since many others support them, they must be valid.

Therefore, the future will demand more differentiation, not less, owing to the proliferation of ideas and narratives coupled with the influential capabilities of governments and large corporations in promoting their agendas via social media. This is a primary motivation behind the writing of this book, as we are presently navigating a world marked by exaggeration and diminishment, and the key to thriving within it lies in embracing differentiation.

Why is differentiation necessary for individuals?

There are several reasons for the importance of differentiation. Firstly, differentiation is an inherent part of daily life, essential for survival. When we wake up in the morning, we differentiate by recognizing differences in our posture, how we are positioned in bed, the need to get up, and the choice of clothing, which is influenced by variations in climate. Additionally, specific commitments or appointments may require us to prepare accordingly. This innate ability to differentiate is crucial for individual survival.

Furthermore, differentiation becomes even more vital to thrive, not just survive. Failure to differentiate can lead to various challenges and complications. Individuals must distinguish right and wrong, determine when and how to communicate effectively and make informed decisions. All these aspects are intricately tied to differentiation.

Consider the example of a student preparing for an exam. Successful exam preparation depends on differentiating relevant and irrelevant material, allocating sufficient time to each subject or topic, and effectively planning study sessions. Again, this underscores the central role of differentiation in various aspects of life.

From a young age and throughout one's life, individuals either implicitly learn about differentiation by observing and mimicking others or are explicitly taught it in educational settings. Even basic math concepts, such as understanding that two plus two equals four and five plus five equals ten, are rooted in differentiation. Success as an individual hinges on the extent to which one embraces and practices differentiation, whether through implicit learning or explicit education.

Why is differentiation necessary for society?

Differentiation is necessary for individuals and society, given that society is composed of individuals. Therefore, it is reasonable to assert that the state of individuals directly affects the state of society. In other words, as individuals go, so goes society. The degree to which individuals practice differentiation directly impacts the health and functionality of our society.

Society, as a collective entity, must actively engage in differentiation. Consider something as fundamental as transportation. None of us would feel comfortable boarding an airplane if pilots, air traffic controllers, ground crews, and mechanics failed to differentiate their roles and responsibilities throughout the process. In aviation, discernment is paramount, ensuring clarity through systems like red lights, yellow lights, and green lights, as well as complex navigational systems.

Moreover, differentiation plays a crucial role in society by distinguishing between individuals of varying ages, such as the elderly and the young. While they may share some everyday needs, their different life stages necessitate different support and care. Therefore, differentiation is an absolute necessity for the functioning of society.

Why is differentiation necessary for relationships?

Relational self-awareness plays a significant role in our relationships with others. It enables us to understand their past, present, and potentially future experiences. This awareness is crucial because relationships often involve expectations and ideals that may not always align with reality. Differentiation becomes essential in relationships as it allows us to recognize the intricate nature of our interactions. It helps us identify the elements that must come together for relationships to flourish.

While the simple directive to "love one another" exists, differentiation acknowledges the complexity inherent in each individual. When both individuals in a relationship practice differentiation, it fosters patience, understanding, a focus on asking questions, and active listening. Consequently, the relationship is more likely to follow a healthier trajectory characterized by holistic support, mutual understanding, and effective partnership.

ACKNOWLEDGMENTS

I would like to thank the God of all wisdom, grace, mercy, patience, faithfulness and love! I agree with this verse "For from him and through him and for him are all things. To him be the glory forever! Amen."

I would like to thank my children who persistently texted, called and pursued me, checkin in on me and encouraging me to keep chasing my purpose. As I wrote in Metamorphic Dictis "one of the most powerful things you can do for a person is look them in the eye and tell them you believe in them".

I would like to thank God for not immediately delivering me out of all the messes I made and for walking with me through this life and allowing me to feel and experience all facets of life. This has given birth to more than I could have ever imagined.

I would like to thank you, the reader for taking your time, which is your most precious commodity, and using it to read this book.

ABOUT THE AUTHOR

Michael is a serial intellectual. He creates intellectual products that transform people and change the world. He was born in Los Angeles and lived there for almost four decades. In 2009, he moved to Baltimore City and has lived there for fourteen years. Michael has five beautiful adult children. Michael has a bachelor's degree in political studies with an emphasis in philosophy as well as a master's degree in divinity.

He is a certified Enneagram administrator, Scrum master and trained in project management. Michael has been coaching and consulting for twenty-five years. He has founded and led multiple nonprofit organizations. Michael is the author of ten books; 100 Meditations: An Everyday Book for Everyday People; Don't Plant, Be Planted; Metamorphic Dictis; Be You; Social Revolution is Baltimore's Only Solution, Hard Questions, Tenses and Limitations and Loses . Michael is also the creator of many personal development tools: Pause exercise, Emotional MRI, and How to Write Strategic Affirmations, The Pillars of Personal Development, The Priority Funnel, Quadrascope, Mirror Exercise and the Life Map.

Michael is an accomplished triathlete and has completed all four distances. Michael's favorite sport is motocross, his favorite fast food is In-N-Out Burger, he is addicted to fresh Reese's Peanut Butter Cups, and absolutely loves rottweilers. His favorite animals are killer whales and tigers. One of his favorite authors is Mark Twain, and one of his favorite quotes from him is "The two most important days of your life are the day you are born and the day you find out why."